Chronic Is The Journey

Processing My Chronic Illness Journey
Through Poetry

Heather Rogers Ivey

BookLeaf Publishing

India | USA | UK

Made with ❤ on the BookLeaf Publishing Platform
www.bookleafpub.in
www.bookleafpub.com

Dedication

To the people around the world who feel alone in their battle with chronic illness and pain. May you feel understood within these pages.

Preface

Throughout my journey I have been diagnosed with a plethora of chronic conditions and although it's nice to have answers, it's a heavy burden to bear when there is no cure. It's overwhelming to know that most people's worst days are your new normal. Being diagnosed with something new is scary, and every single time I collected a new diagnosis, I turned to the chronic illness community. Witnessing people share their stories, I felt seen. Like there are actually people out there who get it. So this is me sharing my story in hopes that it will resonate with the people who need it.

Acknowledgements

Huge shout out to my husband Auston. This book would not exist if it weren't for him. He is my biggest cheerleader and his pep talks give me life. He has been to countless doctors appointments, helped me recover from surgery and other procedures, and comforts me when the pain is all consuming. Not only has he been incredibly loving through every phase of this journey, he also eagerly listened to each new poem and hyped me up every single time. His unwavering belief in me is unmatched and I definitely wouldn't be putting myself out there like this if it weren't for him.

I've also got to shout out my girl CeCe for gifting me a copy of "The Madness Vase" by Andrea Gibson. It was this act of kindness that ignited my passion for poetry and inspired me to start writing poems of my own.

Unanswered Questions

I will never forget the day
I felt the lightning pain
That took my livelihood away

Nothing's been the same

With my feet in stirrups I lay
Can someone please explain?
Am I going to be okay?
I don't mean to complain
It's normal for women they say
Don't be a drama queen
Here's your bill, don't forget to pay
But hey, we're on your team

Nothing to keep the pain at bay
Except sweet Mary Jane
Doctor after doctor I'd pay
For someone to explain
Am I going to be okay?
Please help I'm being slain
For real concrete answers I pray
Can someone please explain?

Am I going insane?

Total Transparency

Feet in stirrups again I lay
Cervical biopsy
They hand me a paper thin sheet
Total transparency
Next is a metal speculum
Sliding in feels icy
A mechanical procedure
A click that feels spicy
Painting insides with vinegar
Explained with courtesy
"That way we can see the changes"
It burns like Hennessy
I stare at the stark white ceiling
Wishing for normalcy
As tears trickle down my cheeks
Stripped of my privacy
"Please take a deep breath and cough"
It takes resiliency
As they hole punch my poor cervix
I start feeling dizzy
Apply paste "to stop the bleeding"
The doc tries to show mercy
As they swab and scrape my insides
I try not to be fussy

Test results in a week or so
I stand and feel tipsy
Then I anxiously wait for an answer
To "Do I have cancer?"

Red Herring

”What great news! You don’t have cancer!”
Those words should make me feel
Exhilirated and hopeful
I must try to conceal
My pain filled desperation
”What about this pain I squeal?”
It’s too intense now to pretend
That none of it is real
The doctor prints me a packet
This all feels so surreal
“Endometriosis” she says
And gives me the whole spiel
My ears are ringing as I leave
Unsure of how I feel
Soon as I’m home I start reading
Start changing my meals
To anti-inflammatory
Hoping it would help heal
But the agony continued
My research would reveal
The gold standard of excision
Dear surgeon take the wheel
Explore and remove if it’s found
And they found a great deal

Said I was rid of the disease
Then sent me home to heal
Only I never got better
Is any of this even real?

In My Head

They say the pain is in my head
And sometimes they are right
I can feel my pulse in my skull
As the lights get too bright
Like a fire inside my retinas
So I turn off the light
And slide into an icy cap
As I open a Sprite
Sipping it to ease the nausea
"Sorry, I can't come tonight"
I text for like the millionth time
Hope it doesn't start a fight
Trying countless medications
Fighting with all my might
As insurance companies deny
I stop being polite
Next we try Botox injections
The improvement is slight
Any relief is better than none
Just want to feel alright
Every three months I shall return
Needles I re-invite
Into my forehead, neck, and shoulders
Clinching my fists tight

Holding my breath with each puncture
Cursing the damn sunlight
I drive home in blinding pain
And turn in for the night

The Fall

I never saw the fall coming
A long way from cloud nine
The cloud I'd floated on for a year
And had finally called it mine

Addicted to euphoria
The shivers down my spine
Couldn't get enough of this high
A feeling so divine

Until ecstasy became agony
Try to pretend I'm fine
But he can see it on my face
"This isn't fair I whine"

The pain doesn't stop when we do
It's on a steep incline
And it wakes me in the night
A loss I can't define

Painsomnia

Tossing and turning for hours
Check the time on my phone
It's 11:05 pm
I roll over and groan
I finally fall asleep again
Then awake to the shank
It's now 12:13 am
And I'm wide awake
Cuz my flank is screaming in pain
Joined by my hip and knee
The loudest choir I've ever heard
It's here to torture me
It doesn't matter how I lay
The pain is here to stay
My body is the queen of swordplay
Please let me sleep I pray
But these prayers remain unanswererd
I check the time again
Ugh you've got to be kidding me
It's not even 1:10
I feel stuck in this endless loop
And all I want is sleep
This vicious cycle wears me down
I roll over and weep

Check the time when my tears are dry
It's now 2:59
And I can't take this shit anymore
Stop trying and resign
I kiss my snoring husband's head
And leave to draw a bath
To emerge my whole body in heat
And to calm down this wrath

Hormonal

I stare at the plant on the desk
Wanting a distraction
Even the statues are pregnant
What a contradiction
Me sitting here with my broken body
Like a sad rejection
Wondering what it must feel like
To not have this affliction
I hear the nurse call out my name
And head in her direction
She tells me to pee in a cup
And leave it at her station
I sit and wonder while I wait
For my next instruction
In walks an energized doctor
To go over my options
If you can even call them that
They have one connection
They are all hormonal treatments
I have an objection
But I don't tell the doctor as
I sit in reflection
Of all the ones I've tried before
That ended in dysfunction

The pill, the shot, the IUD
Oh and the Nuvaring
"So what'll it be?" she asks me
My hands are getting clammy
"Well I guess I can try the patch"
She springs into action
Excitedly writing the script
While giving me instructions
But all it did was make me sick
Just like my prediction

Making It Through

I've only been here for an hour
I've got to keep going
But I'm running out of power
My movements are slowing

The lights above my desk are off
And my fan is blowing
To counteract the heating pad
But the pain keeps growing

By lunchtime I'm in the bathroom
Discreetly throwing up
And giving myself a pep talk
Cuz I must keep going

Snag an ice cap from the freezer
I'm beat and it's showing
Return to my desk and sign in
Curse the monitor for glowing

Sip my tea to calm my stomach
Trying to keep going
As my check engine light flashes
I try to keep from frowning

Cuz I've got to earn a paycheck
But I feel like I'm drowning
I still have two hours to go
But who the fuck's counting

I'm wearing my third ice cap today
And I feel like fainting
Come on you're almost there I say
You've got it, keep going

By the time I clock out from work
The drive home seems daunting
An hour in the heat in traffic
Is just plain tormenting

And the truly horrific thing?
Tomorrow I wake up and do it again.

To Go or Not To Go

Half asleep I crawl out of bed
And I notice it fast
A painful tingle in my legs
That I didn't think would last
So I went to work anyway
Feeling utterly gassed
As my legs filled with lead
"I can't do it" I gasped
As I finally decided
That the pain had surpassed
Anything I'd ever felt before
And it was seeming to last
There in the emergency room
The world felt awfully vast
With so many people in pain
I wasn't an outcast
All of my tests came back normal
Leaving me aghast
Sent home without answers
Like every time in the past

Dropped Plates

I used to love balancing plates
I thrived on being busy
Always wanting to do it all
Silence made me uneasy

I was working a full time job
And pursuing my studies
Dreaming of writing and editing
Plus I was volunteering

Trying to make a difference
I know it sounds cheesy
But I had to give it all up
One by one wasn't easy

First I quit my volunteer job
Just for now I thought
Until my health improves I said
Now I've stopped holding my breath

The next plate I dropped was school
Cuz the world is greedy
And I now had medical bills
Pilling up like crazy

I knew I couldn't lose my job
But the days became hazy
As I held on for dear life
And tried to keep busy

Despite my efforts I burned out
Daily feeling drowsy
Desperatly wanting to give up
Cried it out in therapy

That's when my therapist told me
To listen to my body
Instead of ignoring it's cries
Regardless of anybody

But the thing is
Listening can also mean
Sacrificing and sometimes
Losing can become a blessing
Even when it's messy

Cane Shame

My first cane came from Amazon
I'd only use it at home
So I never left on the days
When I needed one
But as my symptoms progressed
I lost my liberty
I could no longer hide away
From this reality
When I was overcome with shame
Denying disability
Auston wrapped his arms around me
And kissed my head gently
Asked, "Does using a cane help you?"
"Yes", I muttered faintly
"Then who gives a fuck what they think?"
That's a mentality
That I have never ever had
But gives me security
And I need to hear it often
To keep my sanity
Being disabled in public
Is a hard thing to do
I notice everyone staring
I'm an animal in a zoo

Caged by the pain in my legs
And the speed at which I move
Which is way too slow for this world
I know they disapprove
I know I'm in everyone's way
So I try to step aside
And I try to move faster
But my poor legs are fried
"Go at your own pace" he will say
Being my loving guide
Like an angel on my shoulder
Who holds me while I cry

The Facade

This isn't my real name
I've been chasing fame
Took my script studied my lines
Put on a show for the times
Poisoned your veins kissed your face
Plotted your fall from grace
What an elaborate hoax
To be the butt of their jokes
Pulled on all your heart strings
Purchased wedding rings
Forever chaining you to me
My loyal servant you shall be
Passionate for power
It's men I devour
Pretending to be helpless
I'm sinister and scandalous
Unquenchable craving
The damsel needs saving
"She's perpetually pleading"
"You really should be leaving"
"Don't look back it's all a trap"
"Your soul she will kidnap"
"Her symptoms must be mental"
"I know she seems gentle"

"Her doctors are all quacks"
"Because none of it tracks"
"Son, you need to run for dear life"
"Please, please, please, don't make her your wife"
I get it, loving me
Is an act of charity
It takes work and it's far from easy
Cuz I'll forever be needy
A medical mystery
With a shady history
Maybe someday I'll have answers
That will silence the doubters
At the end of the day
Your decision was made
You chose this life with me
Because the person that you see
Is me through and through
You still see my value
And know my heart is true
For that, I thank you

Racehorse

Mid-afternoon, mid-June
Old car with no AC
Dreaded post work commute
Windows down hot air
My head is a balloon
The sun's blinding glare
Put up my hair
Spray myself with water
None of this is rare
The heat is suffocating
I'm hungry for air
I feel like fainting
I continue spraying
For the momentary
Chill that keeps me going
My heart is a racehorse
She's the fastest in the heat
With mighty hooves of force
She goes so fast
I get knocked on my ass
As she gallops past
Kicking up dust in my brain
Forming thick clouds that...
Sorry, I lost my train...

I hear hoof beats in my head
Clock them at 139 BPM
Guess it's time to crawl in bed

Rare

All I ever wanted to be was
Special
But I learned that blending in is
Beneficial
Karaoke kid who had to turn
Inward
Became versed in hiding pain from the
World
Spending all my energy to seem
Normal
A good girl, a perfect little
Angel
A warm inviting beach scene on the
Screen
Unaware of the horrors that remain
Unseen
When you are the only one who
Sees
Will you ever be
Believed?
Did you know the rarest mineral
On Earth
Has pain in it's name and that hasn't decreased
It's worth?

People are fascinated by something
Rare
But captivation doesn't come with
Care
To be rare is to be
Misunderstood
For no one to see the pain you've
Withstood
And if no one ever sees
It
Does it even
Exist?

Fresh Bulbs

I always change the bulbs
Before they burn out
Because I must make sure
They don't go out at night
And give my loved ones a fright
For they can never know
The depths of this darkness
Trapped in the cage of my anatomy
As it perpetually tortures me
A prisoner who appears to be free
Bound by destiny
There is no escape for me
But the lights still glow
Because they can never know
What it has done to my soul
Or how dark it gets
When the lights go out

The Stars In My Sky

I know it's hard my love
To see me in so much pain
Pain that changes and morphs
Yet never subsides
What's mine is yours after all
I feel it and in a way you do too
As you search for a solution
A way to make it all better
You're not afraid
To take on the impossible
Look it in the face and say
"Challenge Accepted"
Only there is no fix
For the things that hurt me
What you can do though
Is place joy in the palm of my hand
Leaving little indentations of happiness
Like the dimples on your cheeks
And the echoes of your laughter
Cradle my fragile heart in your arms
Like a newborn baby
Turn my tears into rain we can dance in
As your lips greet mine
What's yours is mine my love

So feel the magic
Laugh louder than you ever have
Let those dimples shine
Because they are the stars in my sky

If I Had a Nickel

It was the third Endo specialist
Who pointed me in the right direction
But only after I refused the hormones
And she expressed her dissatisfaction
"Try it and if your symptoms don't improve
We'll know Endo is out of the question"
I wonder how this makes any sense
"Although I have a strong suspicion"
She rattles off the name quite quickly
And sends me to the check out station
The world around me feels muffled
As I repeat the name with determination
The words were foreign to me
But I was assigned to this mission
So I must see it through
Even when I've lost my vision
And when hope feels worlds away
Because of an allergic reaction
That robbed me of a solution
And left me with no option

For Better or Worse

I have my veins to blame for my pain
Extra veins means extra pains
I'm an anomaly
An episode of Chicago Med
At least it's not all in my head
I'm presented with two cases
Deal or No Deal
Impossible choices
For better or worse
Is a mystery
Choose wisely of course
If you choose wrong
More pain you shall gain
But hey, you're strong
Worse is something I can't fathom
What a wretched word
And the most dreadful outcome

Dynamic

Why is it called a dynamic disability?
Is it because the pain hits with such force
That it knocks my power out?
Because it's so loud that it drowns
Out the rest of me?
It throws me into the rip current
And drains the strength from my limbs
As my insides are shredded to bits
A week later I wash up on the shore
With burned skin and exhaustion
Just so I can do it all over again

Lost At Sea

Lost at sea
Unable to find the shore
The water is getting deeper
I'm treading with all I have
To keep from drowning
I can't feel my legs anymore
Tired of waiting for rescue
That's never going to come
Dehydrated of hope
Afraid of the vastness
And the monsters within
How do you keep going
When everything is out of reach
And there's no one who can save you?

Irish Goodbye

Goodbye sweet girl
From the rock shows
Who lived for Warped Tour
And rallied for Riot Fest
So she could see all her faves
In one long epic weekend
The girl who blew all her money
on concert tickets
A decade ago
The girl who crowd surfed
Met the bands
Stood front row
Joined the pit
Chased the feeling of being alive
I never knew I'd miss her
Never thought she'd Irish Goodbye